Lena Anlauf & Vitali Konstantinov

GENIUS EYES

A Curious Animal Compendium

Translated from the German
by Marshall Yarbrough

North South

LOOK!

GIANT EYES
Colossal squid 6 Vampire squid 6 Emperor dragonfly 7 Common ostrich 7 Bigeye thresher 7 Margay 8 Colugos 10 Night monkeys 12 Lorisids 14 Tarsiers 16 Owls 18 Eagles 19 Urutau 20

TALKING EYES
Bearded vulture 22 Gee's golden langur 23 Flashlight fish 23 Barbeled dragonfish 23 Guppies 23 Chameleons 24

ACCESSORIZED EYES
Secretary bird 26 Southern ground hornbill 26 Giraffe 26 Wild Bactrian camel 26 Eyelash viper 26 Eyelash gecko 26 Yellow-eyed penguin 27 Swallow-tailed gull 27 Schlegel's asity 27 Porcupine fish 27 Red-shanked douc 27 European wildcat 27 Blue-eyed spotted cuscus 27 Blue-eyed black lemur 27

ADAPTABLE EYES
Swordfish 28 Pacific barreleye fish 28 Strawberry squid 28 Reindeer 29 Western parotia 29 Olm 29

MASKED EYES
Penduline tit 30 White-crested laughingthrush 30 Dusky leaf monkey 30 Raccoon 30 Black-footed ferret 30 Numbat 30 Rufous motmot 30 Brown-throated sloth 30 African penguin 30 Meerkat 31 Giant panda 31 Lion 31

Teary eyes
Broad-snouted caiman 32 Arrau turtle 32 Kirk's dik-dik 32
Barn owl 33 Blue-and-yellow macaw 33 Red-footed tortoise 33
Roadside hawk 33 Loggerhead sea turtle 33 Green sea turtle 33

Super pupils
Flame bowerbird 34 Mauritius ornate day gecko 34 Eyelash leaf-tailed gecko 34 Yellow-bellied toad 34 White-spotted bush frog 34 Chamois 35 Four-eyed fish 35 Common cuttlefish 35 Hummingbird hawk-moth 35 Malaysian shield mantis 35

Many eyes
Red wood ant 36 European mantis 36 Hornet 36 American cockroach 36 Large red damselfly 36 Western honeybee 36 Hairy whirligig beetle 36 Coastal peacock spider 37 Atlantic horseshoe crab 37 Atlantic bay scallop 37 Iguanas 38

Stalked eyes
Hammerhead shark 40 White-lipped snail 41 Vomer conch 41 Horn-eyed ghost crab 41 Stalk-eyed fly 41 Peacock mantis shrimp 41

Scary eyes
Peacock butterfly 42 Peacock day gecko 42 Four-eyed turtle 42 Peacock eel 42 Copperband butterflyfish 42 Crab-eyed goby 42 Ambon damselfish 42 Cuyaba dwarf frog 43 Mountain pygmy owl 43 *Hemeroplanes triptolemus* caterpillar 43 Texas horned lizard 43 Red-eyed tree frog 44

Appendix
Glossary 47 Note 50 Sources 51 Index 52

GIANT EYES

The basketball-sized eyes of the giant squid and colossal squid are the largest in the world! Squid use them to see in the lightless depths of the deep sea, always on the lookout for their mortal enemy: the sperm whale! The sperm whale itself doesn't glow, but the smaller deep-sea creatures that swim alongside it do, and they create a twinkling silhouette. Squid can see these whale-shaped clouds of light from more than a hundred meters (three hundred feet) away —and take them as a sign to flee.

Many animals' eyes will give some indication of where they live or what time of day they are active. Nocturnal animals and animals that live in the deep sea often have large eyes with giant pupils that are very sensitive to light.

The largest eyes relative to body size belong to the tiny vampire squid—they make up almost one-sixth of its length! The vampire squid uses its giant eyes to find its favorite meal: carrion, which often teems with bacteria that give off a faint glow.

Emperor dragonfly

The insect with the largest eyes is the dragonfly. Its two giant compound eyes are composed of up to 30,000 tiny little eye units! These units are called ommatidia.

The eyes of the common ostrich can measure up to five centimeters (two inches) across! That makes them the largest eyes of all land animals. Thanks to its big eyes, the flightless bird is able to spot its predators in time and run away across the savanna, reaching speeds of up to seventy kilometers (forty-three miles) per hour.

The largest fish eyes, measuring more than ten centimeters (four inches) across, belong to the bigeye thresher!

7

MARGAY
Leopardus wiedii

Margays live in the tropical rain forests of Central and South America. As is common among predator animals, they have forward-facing eyes. This makes them especially good at gauging distances, which helps these large-eyed felines to live and hunt in the trees. They are extremely adept climbers: margays can run down a tree trunk headfirst and hang down from a branch using just their back paws to hold on.

CAT'S EYE

Margay eyes have a reflective layer behind the retina: the *tapetum lucidum*. When light hits this layer, the tissue reflects it back, amplifying the light and further stimulating the photoreceptor cells in the eye. You can observe this effect in house cats as well: if a light shines on a cat's eyes in the dark, they will begin to glow.

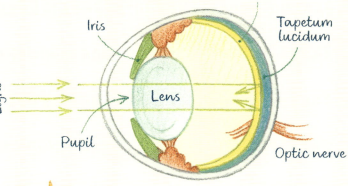

At night the margay's pupils become greatly enlarged. This allows more light to enter the eye, which becomes more sensitive—better for seeing in the faint light of the moon. When margays are out during the day, however, their pupils shrink down to narrow slits. That way they don't get blinded by the sunlight.

Sunda flying lemur

COLUGOS
Dermoptera

Colugos are an order of gliding mammals with two species: the Philippine flying lemur and the Sunda flying lemur. Both make their homes in the tropical rain forests of Southeast Asia. Colugos' closest relatives are primates. When they aren't gliding, they hang out in the trees and have a sloth-like way of moving.

Colugos' bulging eyes are sensitive to light and help the nocturnal animals see in the dark.

With a large membrane of skin along their sides as well as webbed fingers and toes, colugos are perfectly adapted for gliding. They can glide for more than 130 meters (430 feet). Their eyes are also specially adapted for gliding: they face forward and have overlapping fields of view. As a result, colugos have particularly good depth perception. They are excellent at gauging the distances between trees, allowing them to land safely.

When two colugos meet, they sometimes stare into each other's eyes for up to an hour. This is how new mates find each other.

NIGHT MONKEYS
Aotidae

Night monkeys are the only nocturnal monkeys in the world! They live in the forests of Central and South America.

Gray-handed night monkey

They are found in small family groups. Usually it's the fathers that carry the young around.

There are different theories as to why night monkeys live in the dark. One is that they save energy by sleeping through the heat of the day; another is that there is less competition at night to find fruit to eat. A third theory is that they are protected from predators that sleep during the nighttime—in places where monkeys might encounter more predators at night, they tend to be active during the day.

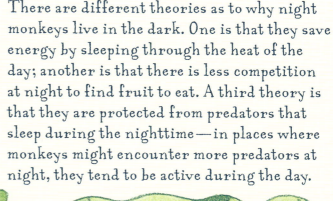

Night monkeys are *monochromats*, meaning they see only one color. They can only perceive different shades of gray. Nevertheless, they see better at night than other monkeys because they have significantly more photoreceptors for seeing in the dark.

On nights when there is a new moon, though, it's too dark even for night monkeys. On such nights they are barely active, although they might follow their noses to feeding spots that they have previously marked with their scent.

Studies featuring different species of monkey have shown that animals that see fewer colors are less likely to be deceived by them: because they are better at detecting shapes, they are quicker to spot prey animals that use color to camouflage themselves.

Red-bellied tamarin

13

Gray slender loris

LORISIDS
Lorisidae

Lorisids are a family of primates found in the forests of Asia and Africa. Slender lorises have the largest eyes among them. Even in the dark of night, they can move sure-footedly along spindly swaying branches.

Pygmy slow loris

Slender lorises

Angwantibos

Slow lorises

Pottos

Lorisidae genera

Lorisids are at risk of going extinct. One reason is that they are illegally sold as pets. It might look cute when they raise their arms over their heads, but it's supposed to be a defense mechanism! They are probably imitating a venomous cobra. Slow lorises are the only primates that can produce their own toxin; they do so by licking a gland on their arm.

Lorisids are outstanding hunters and rely almost completely on their eyes. Like margays, lorisids have forward-facing eyes that are equipped with a *tapetum lucidum*.

Like most mammals, lorisids are *dichromats*: that means they can see two colors but can't perceive the color red. You can use red light to observe them in the dark without blinding them. Most lorisids show no fear of observers; they just stare back with their head cocked to one side.

15

Horsfield's tarsier

TARSIERS
Tarsiidae

Tarsiers are a family of primates with fourteen known species. They live in the understory of tropical rain forests in maritime Southeast Asia. The smallest among them is the pygmy tarsier, considered by some scientists to be extinct—it's been decades since anyone has seen one.

TARSIER SKULL

The Horsfield's tarsier has the largest eyes relative to body size of any mammal. If people had tarsier eyes, they would be as big as grapefruits!

The first thing you notice when you see a tarsier skull is the giant eye sockets. The tarsier can't move its eyes—they always stare straight ahead. This trait is one that the tarsier has in common with the owl, and, like owls, tarsiers have remarkably flexible necks. The tiny tarsier can rotate its head about twice as far as a human can: roughly 260 degrees.

Tarsiers are the only primates that eat exclusively meat. To find prey at night, they listen to their surroundings. When they've located something to eat, they use their giant eyes to determine precisely how far away it is—then they pounce!

OWLS

Burrowing owl

Tawny owl

There are about two hundred different species of owl worldwide. Most of them hunt for prey at night, though some owls are active at dusk or during the day. These owls have yellow or orange eyes. Dark eyes, on the other hand, tend to be an indicator of nocturnal behavior.

Instead of round eyeballs, owls have cylindrical eyes that extend far back into their heads: if you look into an owl's ears, located on either side of its head, you can see the backs of its eyes. The telescope-like shape helps owls see astoundingly well even without a lot of light.

Owls' eyes are huge relative to the size of their body. Like all birds, they can barely move their eyes, but to look at their surroundings they can turn their heads almost all the way around—up to 270 degrees!

Because both of an owl's eyes face forward, they have very keen depth perception.

Northern white-faced owl

When a northern white-faced owl feels threatened, it opens its eyes wide and aggressively fans out its feathers. If, however, the owl judges the animal it's facing to be stronger, it quickly tries to camouflage itself, becoming as slim as possible and narrowing its eyes down to inconspicuous slits.

EAGLES

Golden eagle

Steller's sea eagle

Eagles can be found on every continent except Antarctica. These large-eyed birds of prey are among the animals with the keenest eyesight. This helps them keep a lookout for prey in mid-flight. In open terrain in daylight, they can spot a grasshopper a hundred meters (330 feet) away, a lizard four hundred meters (1,300 feet) away, and a rabbit at least a thousand meters (3,300 feet) away. They can't see much in the dark, though.

Eagle eyes see *superfast*: they can see far more frames per second than humans can. As a result, even when diving to catch their prey, they keep everything in sight.

A bony ridge over the eyes gives eagles their grim raptor's look. This feature protects their sensitive eyes from injuries they might sustain from diving into brush while hunting for prey. It also shields their eyes from the sun when scanning the ground for prey on bright days.

URUTAU
Nyctibius griseus

The urutau, also known as the common potoo, is found in Central and South America. During the day it disguises itself as a tree trunk, perching upon a stump, sticking its beak up in the air and then sitting there, motionless. This way it seems to blend in with the bark of the tree.

A potoo mating pair produces just one egg per year. During the day the male broods the purple-spotted egg; at night, the female does.

With its giant eyes, the potoo has fantastic night vision. When hunting for insects, it opens its short beak super wide. This, along with its ghostly song—*BOO-OU-OU-OU-OU-OU*—earned it the name *urutau*, which means "ghost mouth" in Guarani.

Even spookier, potoos can see with their eyes closed! They have two (or sometimes three) notches in their eyelids that allow them to watch their surroundings through closed eyes. Thanks to this adaptation, they can spot potential predators without opening their eyes, which are so conspicuous that they would spoil their disguise. The feathers around the eyes are also flattened, so they don't block the bird's view.

TALKING EYES

Many animals use their eyes to communicate. Sometimes the message is conveyed by the eyes themselves. Other times they perceive a message expressed via light or color, directed from one individual to another of the same species.

Bearded vultures are found in Africa, Asia, and Europe. With a wingspan of nearly three meters (ten feet), they are some of the largest birds capable of flight in the world! Their vision is excellent, but their eyes have another peculiar feature: the scleral ring, a bony support around the iris. You can tell what mood the bearded vulture is in by looking at this ring—when the vulture is agitated or excited, it turns dark red, thanks to the increased flow of blood.

Gee's golden langur

You can read the mood of most mammals by looking at their eyes, which reveal if the animal is excited, afraid, or curious. A threatening stare indicates aggression. Where an animal is looking can also reveal where its attention lies. Consciously looking in a specific direction can act as a gesture, like pointing your finger.

Some species light up so that they can see each other in the dark! This is called bioluminescence, and it has many uses, including communication between individuals of the same species.

Flashlight fish, for example, flash messages back and forth with the help of luminous bacteria that live in a pouch below their eyes. A quick flash means danger.

Barbeled dragonfish have their own luminous cells. By emitting blue light they lure prey, and by emitting red light they can stealthily illuminate their surroundings—because hardly any other deep-sea creature can see red.

Guppies have a silver iris that darkens when they're spoiling for a fight.

23

Almost half of the more than two hundred chameleon species in the world are found on Madagascar. Chameleons have especially keen eyesight, and their eyes are unique: they can move independently of one another and bulge far out of their sockets. The upper and lower eyelids are fused together and cover the eye almost entirely, except for a small hole.

Chameleons can tell what mood other chameleons are in from their skin coloration, and convey their own messages in the same way. Males in search of a mate are particularly colorful. Otherwise, coloration mostly serves camouflaging purposes: tree-dwelling chameleons are often green, while those that live on the ground are brown.

Brown leaf chameleon under a black light

During the day, chameleon eyes can produce droplets of oil that act like sunglasses! At night, however, chameleons can hardly see a thing.

Chameleons are *tetrachromats*. That means they can see four colors, including ultraviolet light. Their bones even reflect ultraviolet light, giving off a blue glow underneath their skin.

Scientists are still trying to find out what purpose these ultraviolet light patterns serve. Maybe they help chameleons recognize one another, or lure insects that can see ultraviolet light....

When hunting for prey, a chameleon looks around with both eyes and alternates its focus between the two fields of view. Once it has spotted an insect, it points both eyes in the same direction, gauges the correct distance, and shoots its projectile tongue out to grab it—with tremendous accuracy.

25

ACCESSORIZED EYES

EYELASHES

Birds that tend to hunt on the ground, like the secretary bird and the southern ground hornbill, have impressive eyelash-like feathers that shield their eyes from both churned-up dust and the sun.

Giraffes have long, highly sensitive eyelashes. When grazing in the trees, their eyelashes warn them when they get too close to thorns and twigs that might damage their eyes. Wild Bactrian camels have a double row of eyelashes to protect their eyes from the sandy dust in their desert habitat.

The eyelash viper and the eyelash gecko have what look like elegant scaly lashes. It's said the venomous viper bats its long lashes at its victims — but snakes don't actually have eyelids.

COLOR RIOT! Many birds have especially colorful eyes! For the most part these are for impressing others of their species: the most popular yellow-eyed penguins are the ones with the brightest, yellowest eyes. The eyes of the Schlegel's asity and the swallow-tailed gull are surrounded by decorative features.

Bright specks of glitter can be seen in the eyes of porcupine fish. These probably act to shade their eyes from overly bright sunlight when they swim close to the water's surface. The fish also get help from the small "sunshade" that juts out over each eye.

Red-shanked doucs are also called makeup monkeys because of the distinctly blue eyelids that stand in sharp contrast to their orange faces. They show off their eyelids to other doucs by playfully batting their eyes at them.

Most mammals living in the wild have brown eyes—but there are a few exceptions.

27

ADAPTABLE EYES

The swordfish has a special trick up its sleeve: in the cold depths of the deep sea, it can warm up its eyes and brain with the help of heater cells. This enhances the organs' performance, allowing the swordfish to see its prey almost in slow motion.

What appear at first glance to be the eyes of the Pacific barreleye fish are actually its nostrils! A barreleye fish swims while looking upward through its transparent head. Inside, the eyes are protected from the stingers of its prey. Scientists learned recently that the position of its eyes is not fixed, so when hunting, the barreleye fish points its eyes forward.

When the strawberry squid first hatches, its two eyes look the same. But then one eye grows significantly faster than the other and develops a shiny yellow-green lens. The strawberry squid usually swims on a slight tilt, using its small eye to watch for bioluminescence below, while its large eye discerns shapes in the murky waters above.

In the northern polar regions where reindeer live, the days are long for most of the summer. Reindeer have golden brown eyes that are less sensitive to light and protect them from being dazzled by the sun.

In the winter, it's dark nearly all the time. During this season, their eyes turn dark blue! With their "winter eyes," reindeer can't see as clearly, but they can see better in the dark.

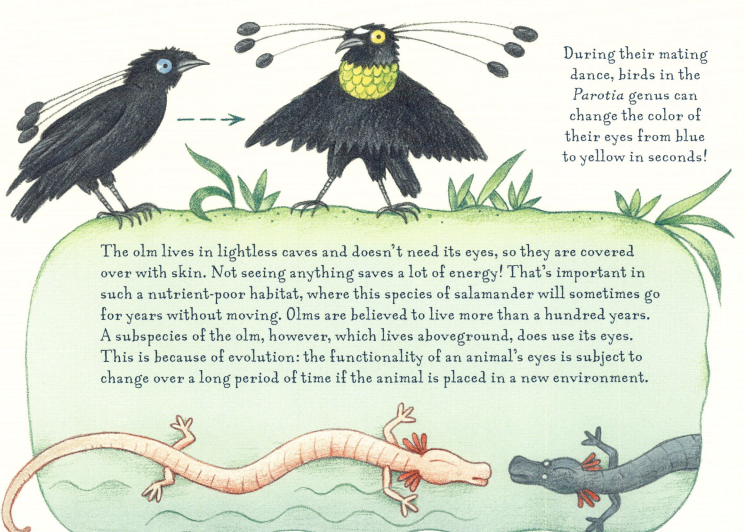

During their mating dance, birds in the *Parotia* genus can change the color of their eyes from blue to yellow in seconds!

The olm lives in lightless caves and doesn't need its eyes, so they are covered over with skin. Not seeing anything saves a lot of energy! That's important in such a nutrient-poor habitat, where this species of salamander will sometimes go for years without moving. Olms are believed to live more than a hundred years. A subspecies of the olm, however, which lives aboveground, does use its eyes. This is because of evolution: the functionality of an animal's eyes is subject to change over a long period of time if the animal is placed in a new environment.

MASKED EYES

Penduline tit
White-crested laughingthrush
Raccoon
Black-footed ferret
Rufous motmot
Numbat
Dusky leaf monkey
Brown-throated sloth

Many animals hide their eyes within dark masks of fur or feathers. Others have light-colored masks, which tend to make their eyes look larger.

African penguins have patches of skin around their eyes that look like glasses. When they get too hot, the birds pump more blood to these featherless patches, which cools them off. You can tell an African penguin is hot if its "glasses" are dark red. If the penguin is cold, the patches turn a pale pink color. African penguins tell each other apart by looking at the pattern of spots on their bellies.

Dark patches of fur or feathers around the eyes can act like sunglasses. They reflect less light and keep meerkats from being dazzled by the sun when keeping a lookout for possible dangers during the day.

Giant pandas recognize their fellow pandas by the masks around their eyes. Each panda's mask is unique.

Lions have a strip of white fur beneath their eyes. This reflects and amplifies residual light to help them see when prowling around at night or at dusk.

31

TEARY EYES

Crocodile and river turtle tears are a happy sight for butterflies and bees: they drink the reptiles' lachrymal fluid, which contains rare nutrients.

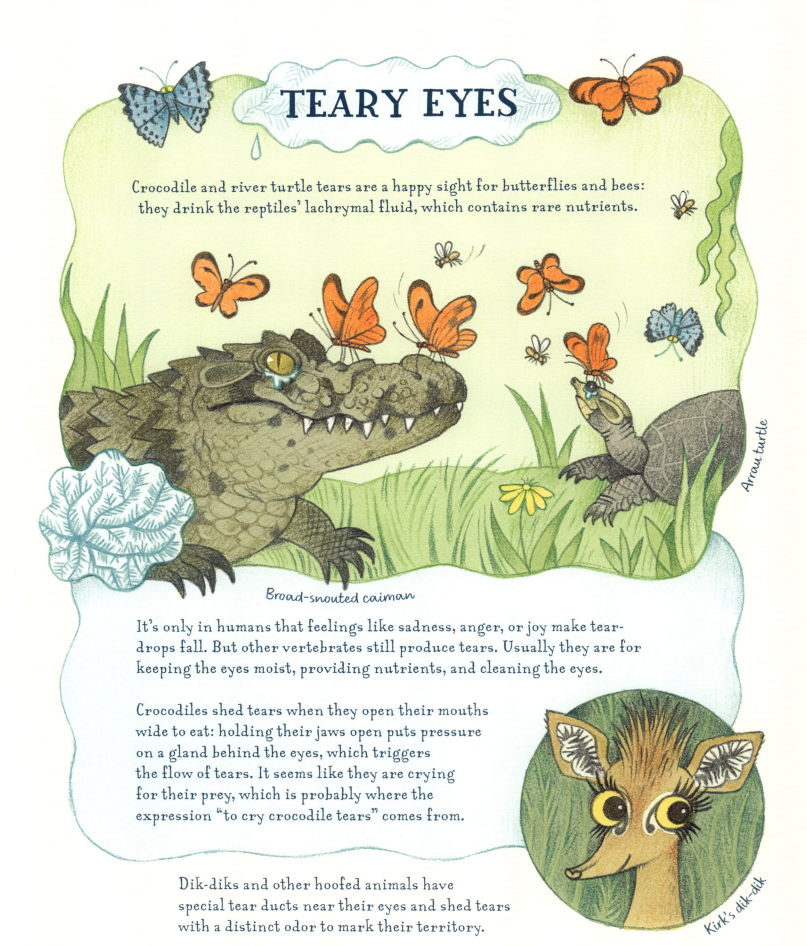

Broad-snouted caiman

Arrau turtle

Kirk's dik-dik

It's only in humans that feelings like sadness, anger, or joy make teardrops fall. But other vertebrates still produce tears. Usually they are for keeping the eyes moist, providing nutrients, and cleaning the eyes.

Crocodiles shed tears when they open their mouths wide to eat: holding their jaws open puts pressure on a gland behind the eyes, which triggers the flow of tears. It seems like they are crying for their prey, which is probably where the expression "to cry crocodile tears" comes from.

Dik-diks and other hoofed animals have special tear ducts near their eyes and shed tears with a distinct odor to mark their territory.

When scientists began studying the lachrymal fluid of various animal species, they found that different animals' tears seemed adapted to the animals' particular habitats: green sea turtles, for example, who live in salt water, have particularly viscous tears.

Barn owl Blue-and-yellow macaw Red-footed tortoise Roadside hawk

Viewed under the microscope, dried tears look like tiny crystal works of art. These tear patterns vary from animal to animal.

Loggerhead sea turtle

Sea turtles seem to cry when laying eggs on the beach — in reality, they are shedding excess salt that they have consumed in the ocean water.

Green sea turtle

SUPER PUPILS

Light passes into the eye through the pupil. Its size is adjusted by the muscles in the iris. In mammals this occurs involuntarily and depends on the brightness of an animal's surroundings or its emotional state. Birds, however, can consciously control the muscles in their irises. Making their pupils bigger or smaller is part of their body language—the flame bowerbird uses this hypnotic technique in its mating dance.

Mauritius ornate day gecko

Eyelash leaf-tailed gecko

Diurnal geckos have round pupils, while nocturnal geckos have slit-shaped pupils. The latter can be widened considerably in the darkness. All pupils are actually round when they reach their maximum size.

All kinds of pupil shapes can be found in the order of frogs:

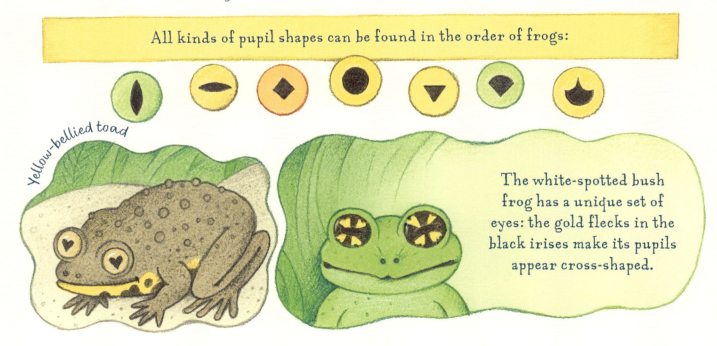

Yellow-bellied toad

The white-spotted bush frog has a unique set of eyes: the gold flecks in the black irises make its pupils appear cross-shaped.

Animals whose defense mechanism is to flee often have wide horizontal pupils and eyes that sit on either side of their head. This gives them a panoramic view of their surroundings, which helps them watch for approaching predators without having to constantly turn their heads and look around. When these animals lower their heads to graze, their pupils rotate and remain horizontal.

Chamois

Four-eyed fish have two eyeballs but four pupils, allowing them to see above water and underwater simultaneously.

Cephalopods like squid have *W*- and *U*-shaped pupils. This shape likely allows them to perceive colors, despite their lack of color-detecting photoreceptors.

Common cuttlefish

Hummingbird hawk-moth

Malaysian shield mantis

The compound eyes of insects often have *pseudopupils* that move in relation to the observer's position. This gives the observer the impression that the insect is watching them.

35

MANY EYES

Most insects are many-eyed in two senses: First, they have two large compound eyes that each consist of thousands of individual units called ommatidia. Second, some of them also have between three and six additional simple eyes, or ocelli. In flying insects, these ocelli are found on the forehead. The insects don't perceive images with them, only changes in light. Ocelli are specially adapted to process visual signals quickly and help the insect keep its balance when airborne. If they are covered, flying insects will tumble and reel.

Red wood ant · European mantis · European hornet · American cockroach · Large red damselfly

Insects don't see especially clearly with their compound eyes. Many of them do see ultraviolet light, however. Pollinators like honeybees and bumblebees perceive inviting patterns on flowers that are invisible to humans.

Western honeybee

Whirligig beetles have compound eyes that are each divided into two parts: one adapted to seeing underwater, one to seeing in the air. This way, as they skim along the water's surface, they can keep their surroundings in view both above and below the water.

Hairy whirligig beetle

36

Coastal peacock spider

Peacock spiders measure just a few millimeters across. Like most spiders they have eight eyes: two principal eyes and six secondary eyes. The principal eyes recognize objects and gauge distances. The secondary eyes have a *tapetum lucidum* and are very sensitive to light. Because of the location on the sides of their heads, they detect almost all movement around the spider.

The mating dances of tiny peacock spider males are impressive!

Horseshoe crabs have ten eyes: two large compound eyes and eight smaller groupings of photoreceptors. They even have photoreceptors on their tails! Scientists are studying the unique qualities of horseshoe crab eyes. Understanding how they work could help humans develop better cameras.

Ocelli
Compound eye
Ocellus
two more ocelli on the ventral side
Photoreceptors
Atlantic horseshoe crab

Scallops have up to two hundred eyes! They are believed to function as motion detectors. They alert the mollusk to the presence of food or warn them of predators.

Atlantic bay scallop

37

IGUANAS
Iguanidae

Iguanas live on rocky terrain, in trees, and on the ground. The more than forty different species of this reptile are found in tropical areas of the Americas and on the islands of Fiji and the Galápagos.

In addition to their two typical vertebrate eyes, iguanas have a third eye on the top of their heads! It's called a parietal eye and is slightly hidden under a transparent scale. Iguanas can perceive light with their third eye and use it to determine the position of the sun, like a combination of clock and compass. It can also help detect movement above the iguana—such as an approaching bird of prey.

Green iguana

Blue iguana

When you pet an iguana's head and cover its parietal eye, it closes its other two eyes and seems to fall asleep.

Male marine iguana with young

The marine iguanas of the Galápagos Islands are the only iguanas that have adapted to dive into the ocean in search of food—in their case algae. This species is usually black in color, like volcanic rock, but come mating season in December the males turn red and green. Hence their other name: Christmas iguanas! The most colorful are considered especially strong.

STALKED EYES

Scalloped hammerhead

The animal kingdom has all different kinds of creatures whose eyes are on stalks. Stalked eyes give these animals a wider field of view. Some hammerhead sharks have eyes set so far apart that they have a vertical panoramic view of their surroundings: they can see potential prey both above and below!

White-lipped snail

Snails of the *Helicidae* family can retract their eyes. They see much more slowly than humans do. To them it looks like we're moving in fast-forward. If a person moves very quickly, snails can't see them at all.

Horn-eyed ghost crab

Vomer conch

If a conch loses one of its stalked eyes, it can grow another within a few weeks.

The horn-eyed ghost crab can fold up its eyestalks for protection before burrowing into the sand.

Instead of fighting to prove their strength, male stalk-eyed flies compare the distance between their eyes: the longer their eyestalks, the more popular they are among the females.

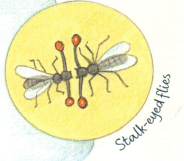
Stalk-eyed flies

Peacock mantis shrimp

Peacock mantis shrimp move their stalked compound eyes around, constantly observing. They have sixteen types of photoreceptors for seeing color—even though four types are enough to perceive the entire color spectrum. The results of one study showed that these shrimp are actually worse at distinguishing colors than other animals with fewer types of photoreceptors. When it comes to detecting primary colors, however, peacock mantis shrimp are especially quick.

41

SCARY EYES

Many animals use eyelike markings called eyespots to appear bigger or meaner than they really are. These markings are mostly for scaring off or confusing potential attackers, and for impressing others of their own species. The peacock has the most well-known and most numerous eyespots; some animals with eyespots were named after the peacock.

Ambon damselfish will develop eyespots on their dorsal fins only if they are in an environment where they frequently encounter predator fish. When the eyespots develop, the fish's actual eyes become correspondingly smaller. This makes it harder for predators to see which direction the fish are fleeing in. Other fish also use this technique to steer predators away from more vulnerable body parts like their heads.

Cuyaba dwarf frogs are known for their distinctive coloration and patterning. They fool predators with the large eyespots on their rear ends. These false eyes also contain poison glands.

Hemeroplanes triptolemus caterpillar

From a distance, the feathery eyespots on the back of the mountain pygmy owl's head look like a menacing stare, warding off unexpected attacks from behind.

A few caterpillars also have false eyes on their rears, which make them look like dangerous venomous snakes.

Some animals use their real eyes to frighten away others. The Texas horned lizard has a special way of defending itself in cases of extreme danger: it can spray blood from its eye sockets at its attacker—and can hit a target accurately from over a meter (three feet) away!

Red-eyed tree frogs are found in the rain forests of Central and South America. They have the largest eyes of any frog, which help guide them as they leap from tree to tree. During the day they sleep, camouflaged on the underside of leaves. When asleep, they can retract their eyeballs. They also lay their spawn on leaves, making sure to choose leaves that hang down over water; when the tadpoles hatch, they drop into the water and start the next stage of their life cycle.

Red-eyed tree frogs even use their eyes to help them swallow! Their eyeballs retract into their skulls, pushing the food farther back into their throat.

Their bright eyes are also used as a warning signal: when they are threatened, they pop their eyes open suddenly. The red color can confuse the attacker for a brief moment and give the tree frog the opportunity to flee.

Nictitating membrane

The red-eyed tree frog, like many other vertebrates, has a nictitating membrane: a third, transparent eyelid that can be drawn protectively over the eye, extending from the middle of the face outward. Covered in a gold-colored mesh, it masks the conspicuously red eyes while still allowing the frog to see through it.

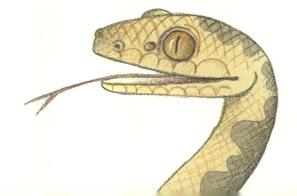

45

GLOSSARY

Color: The ability to see color is individual and varies from animal to animal. Color is what the eyes perceive when light falls on an object and is reflected back. Animals with more types of cone cells in their eyes usually see a wider spectrum of colors, but there are exceptions and different strategies for perceiving color, for example with different pupil shapes.

Compound eye: A visual organ that is found in insects and crabs, it is made up of up to tens of thousands of individual units called ommatidia. Animals with compound eyes don't have particularly sharp vision, but flying insects with compound eyes see "faster" than other animals, meaning they process visual information more quickly.

Depth perception: When an animal has at least two functioning eyes, it has better depth perception when their two fields of view overlap. That means that the animal is better able to gauge distances between objects. The brain makes this possible by combining the information from both eyes. If the eyes face forward, the area in which their fields of view overlap—and thus the area in which the animal has binocular vision—is larger. See diagram on page 48.

Dichromat: An animal that can see two colors. *Chroma* means "color"; *Di* means "two." Dichromats have two different kinds of photoreceptors for seeing color. These are called cones. Unlike dichromats, monochromats only see different shades of gray. Most humans are trichromats and have three types of cone cell for perceiving red, green, and blue, which can combine to form other colors. Some humans, however, like most other mammals, have only two types of cone cell. For these people it can be more difficult to distinguish between red and green—but compared to people with three types of cone cell they sometimes find it easier to discern shapes and see in dim light. Tetrachromats, such as insects or chameleons, also see ultraviolet light. Some trichromats like bees see ultraviolet light too, but besides that they can see only blue and gray.

Evolution: The change of a species' hereditary traits over several generations, often caused by small adaptations that provide a survival advantage within the species' environment.

Eye: A sensory organ that perceives light. Light enters the eye through a transparent lens. In front of the lens is the iris, which, by dilating and contracting the pupil, controls how much light enters the eye. After passing through the lens, the light hits the retina. There it is converted into signals that are transmitted to the brain via the optic nerve. Only when it reaches the brain, and specifically the visual cortex, does the information become the image that one sees. See diagram on page 9.

Eyelashes: Sensitive hairs arranged in rows around the eyes that offer protection to mammals from dust, sunlight, rain, and other irritants. Some birds have feathers that perform the same function.

Eyelids: Eyelids protect the eyes, keep them moist, and shade them from light. Many animals have two eyelids, an upper and a lower, and a few even have three, if you count the nictitating membrane. Some animals that don't have movable eyelids, including some lizards, most geckos, and snakes and fish, have *brilles* instead. A brille is a transparent scale covering the eye and is formed from the upper and lower eyelids fusing together; the word comes from the German word for eyeglasses. Animals with brilles often use their tongues to clean them and keep them moist.

Field of view: An animal's field of view is made up of everything it sees when it moves its eyes but not its head. It is dependent on the placement, number, and motility of its eyes. See diagram below.

Gland: An organ that produces a particular substance and secretes it inside or outside the body.

Hunter eyes: The eyes of predator animals face forward and allow for good depth perception. The eyes of prey animals, by contrast, are usually placed on either side of their head and give the animals a panoramic view of their surroundings. But there are exceptions: herbivorous colugos, for example, have a smaller field of view but good depth perception.

Iris: The iris is a colored diaphragm, impenetrable to light, and full of muscles that control the size of the pupil. See diagram on page 9.

Light: A sensory stimulus that is caused by an energy source, for example the sun. A portion of the energy the sun radiates is visible to humans and animals. Shortwave ultraviolet light and long-wave infrared light can be seen by humans only with the help of specialized cameras or other tools. Some animals, like birds and insects, can perceive ultraviolet light. Snakes such as the eyelash viper can see infrared light with the help of special pit organs located near their eyes. Humans perceive infrared light as warmth. See diagram on page 50.

Mating dance: When one animal, typically a male, attempts to impress a potential mate by putting on a special display.

Monochromat: An animal that sees only one color; see *Dichromat*.

Motion perception: The capacity to see movement, for example to detect predators or prey. See also *Visuospatial processing speed*.

Nictitating membrane: Also called the third eyelid, it is a fold of skin that can be pulled over the eye laterally, moving outward from the middle of the face. Many vertebrates have nictitating membranes and use them to protect their eyes when hunting or diving, or, more generally, from dirt. For polar

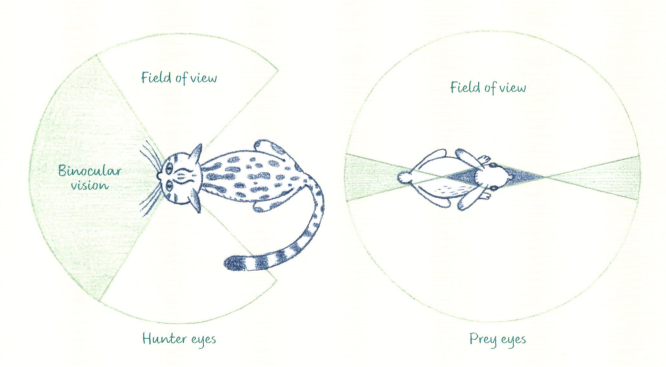

Hunter eyes

Prey eyes

48

bears, the membranes act like sunglasses. The nictitating membrane is usually transparent but nevertheless limits the sharpness of vision. See diagram on page 45.

Ocellus (plural: ocelli): Also called a simple eye, it usually has a retina for perceiving light. In some animals it is more fully developed and also contains a lens.

Panoramic view: A wide-format view of an animal's surroundings that shows little above and below but lots on either side.

Predator: An animal that hunts and eats a prey animal.

Prey: An animal that is hunted and eaten by a predator.

Pseudopupils: The individual units that make up the compound eyes of invertebrates like insects and crabs don't reflect light frontally. This results in the appearance of black spots, called pseudopupils, which move in relation to an observer's position, making it seem as though the eyes are staring back at them. Pseudopupils tend to be more sharply defined after an animal molts its skin.

Pupil: The black opening in the middle of the eye. Light enters the eye through the pupil. In most animals, the pupil's size is controlled by the muscles in the iris — some animals can do this consciously, while for others it's fully automatic. A small pupil lets in only a little light. This is practical if the sun is blindingly bright, but not so good if the surroundings are dim. For that reason the pupil is usually large in the dark: the wider opening lets more light through. At these times the eye is especially sensitive to light and can perceive even a faint glow. See diagram on page 9.

Sight: Perception of light, usually understood as the ability to recognize shapes and colors and to detect movement.

Tapetum lucidum: Also called the tapetum, it is a reflective layer located within or behind the retina. By reflecting the light that passes into the eye, it doubles the stimulus to the retina, thus amplifying residual light. Many nocturnal animals have one in each eye. If you shine a light in the dark on an animal with tapeta, you can see the reflected light shine back through its pupils. See diagram on page 9.

Tears: A bodily fluid, also known as lachrymal fluid, that is usually secreted by tear ducts near the eyes. There are three different types of tears: *Basal tears* moisten the eye and provide it with nutrients. *Reflex tears* wash out foreign objects. *Emotional tears* are a phenomenon known only to humans. The composition of tears, and thus their crystallization pattern, differ depending on the animal that sheds them and the stimulus that triggers them. A lack of lachrymal fluid can lead to blindness.

Tetrachromat: An animal that can see four colors, including ultraviolet light; *see Dichromat*.

Ultraviolet (UV) light: Shortwave light that lies above the spectrum of light visible to humans. Some animals can perceive ultraviolet light. Primates and many other animals have pigmented lenses that block ultraviolet light from entering the eye — ultraviolet light can be harmful, and unprotected exposure to it can also lower visual acuity. With the help of special UV lamps (black lights), people are able to see, if not the UV light itself, then at least the fluorescent glow of chameleon bones or the patterns flowers use to attract pollinators.

Vertebrate: Birds, mammals, reptiles, amphibians, and fish are all vertebrates, meaning they have a skeleton with a spinal column. Nearly all vertebrate animal eyes function in a similar manner.

Visual acuity: The eye's ability to discern patterns and details in well-lit surroundings. When it comes to sharpness of vision, humans are second only to certain species of birds like eagles and hawks. All other animals see less clearly in good light conditions.

Visual field: Includes everything an animal sees when it moves neither its eyes nor its head. It is dependent, among other things, on the number of eyes an animal has and the diameter of its pupils.

Visuospatial processing speed: How "fast" an animal sees is determined by how quickly it processes visual stimuli and can be measured in terms of how many frames per second it perceives. Flying insects see fastest of all. Movements that might seem quick to our eyes will appear to occur in slow motion to a fly. On the other hand, if you move very slowly, a fly can barely perceive your movements. Snails see very slowly—to them, we humans seem to move in fast-forward.

NOTE

World Map: The map at the very front of the book is modeled on the AuthaGraph world map developed by the Japanese architect Hajime Narukawa, currently the most accurate representation of the earth's land masses and bodies of water. The more well-known depiction of the earth based on Gerhard Mercator's rendering from the sixteenth century is far removed from reality. Because the earth is spherical (or close to it), its image always appears distorted on a flat map: in the Mercator projection, Greenland, for example, appears to be about the same size as Africa, even though the continent is in fact almost fourteen times bigger than the island.

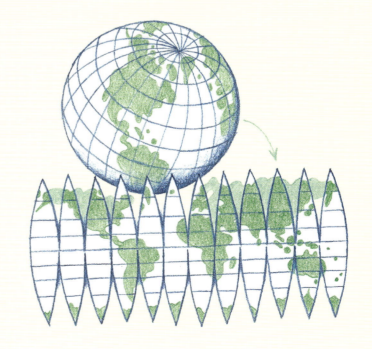

SOURCES

The information in this book is taken from various sources: *Handbook of the Mammals of the World* edited by Don Ellis Wilson and Russel Mittermeier (nine volumes, 2009-2019); *Handbook of the Birds of the World* edited by Josep del Hoyo, Andrew Elliott, Jordi Sargatal, and David A. Christie (sixteen volumes, 1992-2013); the monographs *Lizards of the World* by Mark O'Shea (2021), *Spiders of the World* edited by Norman I. Platnick (2020), and *Turtles of the World* by Jeffrey E. Lovich and Whit Gibbons (2021); *Die Sinne der Tiere* by Stephan Frings (2021); and the study "The mechanistic, genetic and evolutionary causes of bird eye colour variation" by Eamon C. Corbett et al. (2023). On certain pages, reference is made to the results of specific studies:

Page 11: "An ethogram construction for the Malayan Flying Lemur (*Galeopterus variegatus*) in Bako National Park, Sarawak, Malaysia" (Dzulhelmi/Abdullah, 2009).

Page 13: "Effect of colour vision status on insect prey capture efficiency of captive and wild tamarins (*Saguinus* spp.)" (Smith et al., 2012).

Page 18: "The evolution of iris color in relation to nocturnality in owls" (Passarotto et al., 2018).

Page 21: "Notes on the Structure of the Upper Eyelid of Potoos (*Nyctibius*)" (Borrero, 1974).

Page 23: "Social signaling via bioluminescent blinks determines nearest neighbor distance in schools of flashlight fish *Anomalops katoptron*" (Jägers et al., 2021); "Red bioluminescence in fishes: on the suborbital photophores of *Malacosteus*, *Pachystomias* and *Aristostomias*" (Herring/Cope, 2005); "Dynamic eye colour as an honest signal of aggression" (Heathcote et al. 2018).

Page 25: *The Biology of Chameleons* edited by Kristal A. Tolley and Anthony Herrel (2013); "Systematics and signalling of madagascan chameleons of the *Calumma nasutum* group" (Prötzel, 2019).

Page 27: "More than just cool shades" (Schwab, 2002).

Page 28-29: "Warm eyes provide superior vision in swordfishes" (Fritsches et al., 2005); "*Macropinna microstoma* and the Paradox of Its Tubular Eyes" (Robison/Reisenbichler, 2008); "Two eyes for two purposes: in situ evidence for asymmetric vision in the cockeyed squids *Histioteuthis heteropsis* and *Stigmatoteuthis dofleini*" (Thomas et al., 2017); "A black, non-troglomorphic amphibian from the karst of Slovenia: *Proteus anguinus parkelj* n. ssp. (Urodela: Proteidae)" (Sket/Arntzen, 1994).

Page 31: "Visuelle Fähigkeiten beim Großen Panda (*Ailuropoda melanoleuca*)" (Dungl, 2007).

Pages 32-33: "Additional observations of lachryphagous butterflies and bees" (De la Rosa, 2014); "Comparison of Electrolyte Composition and Crystallization Patterns in Bird and Reptile Tears" (Oriá et al., 2020); "Comparative Analysis of Tear Composition in Humans, Domestic Mammals, Reptiles, and Birds" (Raposo et al., 2020).

Page 34: "A closer look at pupil diversity and evolution in frogs and toads" (Cervino et al., 2021).

Page 40-41: "Enhanced visual fields in hammerhead sharks" (McComb/Tricas/Kajiura, 2009). "A Different Form of Color Vision in Mantis Shrimp" (Thoen et al., 2014).

Page 42: "Predator-induced changes in the growth of eyes and false eyespots" (Lönnstedt et al., 2013).

INDEX

C = Cover, S = Spine, B = Back cover

Agalychnis callidryas	Red-eyed tree frog	44, 45, 46
Aglais io	European peacock	42
Ailuropoda melanoleuca	Giant panda	31
Alopias superciliosus	Bigeye thresher	7
Amblyrhynchus cristatus	Marine iguana	38, 39
Anableps anableps	Largescale four-eyes	35
Anax imperator	Emperor dragonfly	7
Anomalops katoptron	Splitfin flashlightfish	23
Aotus azarae	Azara's night monkey	12
Aotus griseimembra	Gray-handed night monkey	13
Apis mellifera	Western honeybee	36
Aquila chrysaetos	Golden eagle	19
Ara ararauna	Blue-and-yellow macaw	33
Arctocebus aureus	Golden angwantibo	15
Argopecten irradians	Atlantic bay scallop	37
Athene cunicularia	Burrowing owl	18
Baryphthengus martii	Rufous motmot	30
Bombina variegata	Yellow-bellied toad	34
Bothriechis schlegelii	Eyelash viper	26
Bradypus variegatus	Brown-throated sloth	30
Brookesia superciliaris	Brown leaf chameleon	C, 24, 25
Bucorvus leadbeateri	Southern ground hornbill	26
Caiman latirostris	Broad-snouted caiman	32
Calumma brevicorne	Short-horned chameleon	25
Calumma gallus	Pinocchio chameleon	24
Calumma parsonii	Parson's chameleon	24
Camelus ferus	Wild Bactrian camel	26
Caretta caretta	Loggerhead sea turtle	33
Cepaea hortensis	White-lipped snail	41
Cephalopachus bancanus	Horsfield's tarsier	16, 17
Chamaeleo calyptratus	Veiled chameleon	24, 25
Chamaeleo chamaeleon	Common chameleon	24
Chelmon rostratus	Copperband butterflyfish	42
Chelonia mydas	Green sea turtle	33
Chelonoidis carbonarius	Red-footed tortoise	33
Conolophus subcristatus	Galápagos land iguana	38
Correlophus ciliatus	Eyelash gecko	26
Creagrus furcatus	Swallow-tailed gull	27
Cyclura lewisi	Blue iguana	39
Diodon holocanthus	Long-spine porcupine fish	C, 27

DRYAS IULIA	*Julia butterfly*	32
EULEMUR FLAVIFRONS	*Blue-eyed black lemur*	27
EUPROTOMUS VOMER	*Vomer conch*	41
FELIS SILVESTRIS	*European wildcat*	27
FORMICA RUFA	*Red wood ant*	36
FURCIFER PARDALIS	*Panther chameleon*	24
GALEOPTERUS VARIEGATUS	*Sunda flying lemur*	10, 11
GARRULAX LEUCOLOPHUS	*White-crested laughingthrush*	30
GIRAFFA CAMELOPARDALIS	*Northern giraffe*	26
GLAUCIDIUM CUCULOIDES	*Asian barred owlet*	C, 3
GLAUCIDIUM GNOMA	*Mountain pygmy owl*	43
GYPAETUS BARBATUS	*Bearded vulture*	22
HALIAEETUS PELAGICUS	*Steller's sea eagle*	19
HEMEROPLANES TRIPTOLEMUS	*Hemeroplanes triptolemus (moth)*	43
HISTIOTEUTHIS HETEROPSIS	*Strawberry squid*	28
IGUANA IGUANA	*Green iguana*	39
LASAIA SULA	*Blue metalmark (butterfly)*	32
LEOPARDUS WIEDII	*Margay*	C, S, 8, 9
LIMULUS POLYPHEMUS	*Atlantic horseshoe crab*	37
LORIS LYDEKKERIANUS	*Gray slender loris*	S, 14, 15
MACROGLOSSUM STELLATARUM	*Hummingbird hawk-moth*	35
MADOQUA KIRKII	*Kirk's dik-dik*	32
MACROGNATHUS SIAMENSIS	*Peacock eel*	42
MACROPINNA MICROSTOMA	*Pacific barreleye fish*	28
MANTIS RELIGIOSA	*European mantis*	36
MARATUS SPECIOSUS	*Coastal peacock spider*	37
MEGADYPTES ANTIPODES	*Yellow-eyed penguin*	27
MESONYCHOTEUTHIS HAMILTONI	*Colossal squid*	6
MUSTELA NIGRIPES	*Black-footed ferret*	30
MYRMECOBIUS FASCIATUS	*Numbat*	30
NYCTIBIUS GRISEUS	*Urutau*	20, 21
NYCTICEBUS COUCANG	*Sunda slow loris*	C, 15
NYCTICEBUS JAVANICUS	*Javan slow loris*	15
OCYPODE CERATOPHTHALMUS	*Horn-eyed ghost crab*	41
ODONTODACTYLUS SCYLLARUS	*Peacock mantis shrimp*	41
ORECTOCHILUS VILLOSUS	*Hairy whirligig beetle*	36
PACHYSTOMIAS MICRODON	*Smalltooth dragonfish*	23
PANTHERA LEO	*Lion*	31
PAROTIA SEFILATA	*Western parotia*	29
PERIPLANETA AMERICANA	*American cockroach*	36
PERODICTICUS EDWARDSI	*Central African potto*	15
PHELSUMA ORNATA	*Mauritius ornate day gecko*	34

Phelsuma quadriocellata	Peacock day gecko	42
Philepitta schlegeli	Schlegel's asity	27
Photostomias atrox	Barbeled dragonfish	B
Phrynosoma cornutum	Texas horned lizard	43
Physalaemus nattereri	Cuyaba dwarf frog	43
Podocnemis expansa	Arrau turtle	32
Poecilia reticulata	Guppy	23
Pomacentrus amboinensis	Ambon damselfish	42
Procyon lotor	Raccoon	30
Proteus anguinus	Olm	29
Ptilopsis leucotis	Northern white-faced owl	18
Pygathrix nemaeus	Red-shanked douc	27
Pyrrhosoma nymphula	Large red damselfly	36
Rangifer tarandus	Reindeer	29
Raorchestes chalazodes	White-spotted bush frog	34
Remiz pendulinus	Penduline tit	30
Rhombodera basalis	Malaysian shield mantis	35
Rupicapra rupicapra	Chamois	S, 35
Rupornis magnirostris	Roadside hawk	33
Sacalia quadriocellata	Four-eyed turtle	42
Sagittarius serpentarius	Secretary bird	26
Saguinus labiatus	Red-bellied tamarin	13
Sepia officinalis	Common cuttlefish	35
Sericulus ardens	Flame bowerbird	34
Signigobius biocellatus	Crab-eyed goby	42
Spheniscus demersus	African penguin	30
Sphyrna lewini	Scalloped hammerhead	40, 41
Spilocuscus wilsoni	Blue-eyed spotted cuscus	27
Strix aluco	Tawny owl	18
Struthio camelus	Common ostrich	7
Suricata suricatta	Meerkat	31
Tarsius fuscus	Makassar tarsier	17
Teleopsis breviscopium	Stalk-eyed fly	41
Trachypithecus geei	Gee's golden langur	23
Trachypithecus obscurus	Dusky leaf monkey	30
Trioceros jacksonii	Jackson's chameleon	24, 25
Tyto alba	Barn owl	33
Uroplatus phantasticus	Eyelash leaf-tailed gecko	34
Vampyroteuthis infernalis	Vampire squid	6
Vespa crabro	European hornet	36
Xanthonycticebus pygmaeus	Pygmy slow loris	15
Xiphias gladius	Swordfish	28

GENIUS NOSES

A Curious Animal Compendium

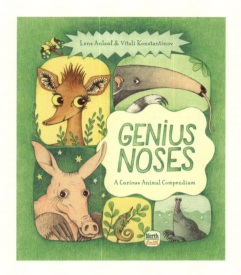

Everything kids ever wanted to know about animal noses around the world! Whether it's the aardvark, the elephant, the pig, or the saiga antelope—they all have wonderful noses. But what can animals do with their noses besides smell?

"A prodigious portrait gallery of prominent proboscises." — **Kirkus Reviews, starred review**

GENIUS EARS

A Curious Animal Compendium

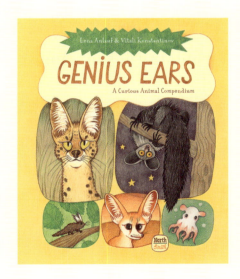

Ears can do much more than just pick up sound waves. In the animal kingdom, ears are sometimes an animal's strongest asset. Long, tuft, or goblin—ears can tell a lot about animals and their habits and habitats.

"Recommended for all elementary, middle school and public libraries. It's attractive, informational, and fun!" —**Youth Services Book Review**

This edition copyright © 2025 by NorthSouth Books, Inc., New York 10016, a subsidiary of NordSüd Verlag AG, Zurich, Switzerland.

Text copyright © 2025 by Lena Anlauf
Illustrations copyright © 2025 by Vitali Konstantinov
English translation copyright © 2025 by Marshall Yarbrough

First published in 2025 in Switzerland by NordSüd Verlag AG under the title *Geniale Augen*.

All rights reserved. No part of this book may be reproduced, transmitted, or utilized in any form, or by any means, electronic, mechanical, photocopying, or otherwise, without the prior written permission from the publisher.

Library of Congress Cataloging-in-Publication Data is available.

Book design by Lena Anlauf & Vitali Konstantinov. Text set in Aunt Mildred MVB, Subtitle, and Gambino. Edited by Lisa Davis.

Printed in Latvia by Livonia Print

ISBN: 978-0-7358-4582-4

1 3 5 7 9 • 10 8 6 4 2

www.northsouth.com

LENA ANLAUF was born in the Ruhr region of Germany. She studied book studies and philosophy in Mainz and Leiden and completed a further education course on pedagogy of literacy and literature as well as a remote course on children's and young adult literature at the STUBE in Vienna. Today she lives in Marburg, works as editorial director and editor at the kunstanstifter verlag, researches historical picture books, and writes and designs her own book projects.

VITALI KONSTANTINOV was born in Ukraine. He studied architecture and art and has taught illustration courses at universities as well as numerous workshops for children. His work has been exhibited extensively, has received many prizes, and has been published in forty different countries. Today Vitali works as a freelance illustrator and author and lives in Marburg. He drew the illustrations for *Genius Eyes* with drawing ink and colored pencil on watercolor paper.